THINK IT, DO IT

HOW TO TURN THOUGHTS INTO MEANINGFUL ACTION

By

Nick Imoru

Achievers Publishing
Calgary, Canada

THINK IT, DO IT: HOW TO TURN THOUGHTS INTO MEANINGFUL ACTION
Copyright © 2024 By Nicholas Imoru

ISBN: 978-1-989291-12-2

Published in Canada, by
Achievers Publishing

Canadian Cataloguing in Publication (CIP)
A Record of this Publication is available from the Library and Archives Canada (LAC).

For further information or permission, address:
Achievers Publishing
Calgary, Canada
E-mail: info@achieverspublishing.com
www.achieverspublishing.com

Printed in Canada for Achievers Publishing

THINK IT, DO IT

HOW TO TURN THOUGHTS INTO MEANINGFUL ACTION

Table of Contents

Contents

INTRODUCTION: THE POWER OF THOUGHT AND THE PITFALLS OF OVERTHINKING

Definition: Think Deeply Versus Overthinking

Thinking deeply is a powerful tool. It involves engaging our minds in a process of reflection, reasoning, and contemplation to gain insights, solve problems, and make sound decisions. Deep thinking allows us to consider different perspectives, analyze situations thoroughly, and draw meaningful conclusions. It is the foundation of critical thinking and creativity, which have been instrumental in shaping innovations, discovering new truths, and finding solutions to complex challenges.

In contrast, overthinking is the act of excessively analyzing or worrying about a problem or situation beyond what is necessary. It often involves rehashing the same thoughts repeatedly without reaching a productive outcome. Overthinking is driven by fear, self-doubt, and the need for perfection. While deep thinking leads to clarity and decision-making, overthinking results in confusion, anxiety, and inaction. Proverbs 12:25 (NIV) states, *"Anxiety weighs down the heart, but a kind word cheers it up."* This verse highlights how overthinking can burden the heart, contrasting with the lightness that comes from thoughtful, positive reflection.

Consider a student preparing for an important exam. Deep thinking helps them analyze the key concepts, understand their application, and develop a study plan. However, if the student begins to overthink, they may worry excessively about failing, dwell on what they don't know, and become overwhelmed by anxiety. Instead of using their time effectively, they get stuck in a cycle of worry and self-doubt, hindering their preparation.

Reframing Overthinking as a Strength

While overthinking is often viewed negatively, it's important to recognize that deep thinking, when channeled correctly, can be a powerful tool. The ability to think deeply allows us to explore complex ideas, consider multiple perspectives, and anticipate potential challenges. When used effectively, this kind of intense reflection can lead to insightful decisions and breakthroughs.

Albert Einstein, who once said, *"It's not that I'm so smart; it's just that I stay with problems longer."* Einstein's deep thinking was key to his scientific discoveries. He often spent long periods contemplating complex problems, exploring all possibilities before arriving at his groundbreaking theories. This is an example of deep thinking at its best—productive and intentional, not hindered by excessive self-doubt or anxiety.

It's crucial to distinguish between deep, productive thinking and unproductive rumination. While deep thinking leads to clarity and problem-solving, unproductive rumination traps us in a loop of self-doubt and worry. The difference lies in the outcome: deep thinking helps us move forward, while rumination keeps us stuck.

A writer planning a novel may spend time deeply contemplating the plot, characters, and themes. This type of reflection helps them create a cohesive and compelling story. On the other hand, if they start second-guessing every detail and worrying about potential criticism, they might fall into the trap of overthinking, which can paralyze their creativity.

In Philippians 4:8 (NIV), we are advised, *"Finally, brothers and sisters, whatever is true, whatever is noble, whatever is right, whatever is pure, whatever is lovely, whatever is admirable—if anything is excellent or praiseworthy—think about such things."* This verse encourages us to focus our deep thinking on positive and constructive topics, rather than allowing our minds to dwell on fear and uncertainty.

When we embrace deep thinking without succumbing to the pitfalls of overthinking, we open ourselves up to new insights and creative solutions. The key is to approach thinking with a sense of curiosity and exploration, rather than fear and worry. By reframing overthinking as a potential strength, we can harness our reflective abilities to make more informed decisions and take purposeful action.

When you find yourself engaged in intense thinking, pause and ask, "Is this helping me move forward, or am I stuck in a loop?" If your thoughts are productive and leading you toward clarity or a solution, embrace them. If they are causing anxiety or indecision, it may be time to shift your focus.

The goal of this book is not to eliminate thinking but to guide readers in recognizing when their reflection is productive and when it becomes detrimental. By understanding the difference, you can use your natural ability to think deeply as a strength rather than a hindrance. This book will equip you with the tools to harness your thoughts effectively, transforming overthinking into meaningful action.

The Purpose of the Book

The purpose of this book is to help readers understand the critical distinction between thinking deeply and overthinking. It aims to provide practical insights and strategies for harnessing the power of thought while avoiding the pitfalls of overanalysis. By exploring real-life examples, scriptural wisdom, and actionable advice, this book will equip readers with the tools they need to cultivate a balanced mindset.

Readers can expect to gain:

- **Clarity** on the difference between productive thinking and overthinking.

- **Practical tools** to identify and break free from the cycle of overthinking.

- **Inspiration** from stories of individuals who have mastered the art of balancing thought and action.

- **Spiritual guidance** through biblical principles that encourage thoughtful reflection and decisive action.

The message is simple yet profound: Thinking is good, but overthinking is not. The goal is to help readers unlock their full potentials by embracing the power of thought without falling into the trap of overthinking.

Philippians 4:8 (NIV) offers a guiding principle for our thought life: "*Finally, brothers and sisters, whatever is true, whatever is noble, whatever is right, whatever is pure, whatever is lovely, whatever is admirable—if anything is excellent or praiseworthy—think about such things.*" This scripture encourages us to focus our thoughts on positive and uplifting things rather than getting bogged down by endless worries and negative analysis.

The Importance of Finding a Balance

The key to a fulfilling and productive life lies in finding the right balance between thoughtful reflection and decisive action. Thoughtful reflection allows us to plan, strategize, and gain understanding, but it must be paired with action to yield results. James 1:22 (NIV) says, "*Do not merely listen to the word, and so deceive yourselves. Do what it says.*" This verse underscores the importance of taking action based on our reflections and insights.

Albert Einstein is a classic example of someone who balanced deep thinking with action. His theories revolutionized our understanding of physics, but they were not just the product of thought experiments; he also conducted research, made calculations, and tested his ideas in the real world. On the other hand, someone who gets trapped in overthinking might spend hours planning without ever implementing those plans, missing out on opportunities for growth and success.

To help readers strike a balance, this book will provide practical steps for:

- Setting realistic goals and deadlines to prevent analysis paralysis.

- Embracing a mindset of experimentation, where mistakes are seen as learning opportunities rather than failures.

- Practicing mindfulness to stay grounded in the present moment, making it easier to transition from thought to action.

The journey of life requires both thought and movement. Thinking is the engine that drives us forward, but without taking steps, we remain in the same place. As we embark on this journey together through the pages of this book, remember that you are not alone. Many have walked this path before, learning to harness the power of their minds while breaking free from the chains of overthinking. Let us explore this balance together, unlocking the potential that lies within a clear, purposeful mind.

CHAPTER 1: THE DIFFERENCE BETWEEN THINKING AND OVERTHINKING

Productive thinking is the ability to engage in a process of reflection and reasoning that leads to clarity, understanding, and meaningful action. It involves analyzing information, considering various perspectives, and making decisions based on well-formed insights. This type of thinking is deliberate, focused, and directed towards solving problems or achieving specific goals.

In Proverbs 4:7 (NIV), it states, "*The beginning of wisdom is this: Get wisdom. Though it cost all you have, get understanding.*" Productive thinking is rooted in the pursuit of wisdom and understanding, helping us navigate life's challenges with clarity and purpose. When we engage in healthy thinking, we allow our minds to explore possibilities, learn from past experiences, and plan effectively for the future.

Consider a business leader faced with making a significant decision. Productive thinking involves analyzing market trends, seeking advice from trusted advisors, and weighing the pros and cons before arriving at a conclusion. This type of thought process is intentional and helps the leader make a decision that aligns with the organization's goals.

The Role of Thoughtful Reflection in Decision-Making

Thoughtful reflection is the practice of pausing to carefully consider one's thoughts, feelings, and experiences before making a decision. It allows us to process our emotions, gain deeper insights, and make well-informed choices. Thoughtful reflection leads to better decision-making because it helps us see the bigger picture and understand the potential consequences of our actions.

In Psalm 119:59 (NIV), the psalmist says, "*I have considered my ways and have turned my steps to your statutes.*" This verse highlights the importance of self-reflection and the willingness to change course when necessary. By taking the time to reflect, we can align our actions with our values and intentions.

To cultivate healthy, productive thinking, try setting aside time each day for reflection. This could be in the form of journaling, meditation, or simply taking a quiet walk. Use this time to process your thoughts, evaluate your goals, and plan your next steps. By doing so, you will develop a habit of deep, purposeful thinking that can guide your decisions.

Now that we've explored what healthy, productive thinking looks like, it's important to understand the key differences between deep, reflective thinking and unproductive overthinking.

Criteria for Recognizing the Shift

Deep thinking and overthinking may appear similar on the surface, but the two have distinct characteristics that set them apart. Here are some key criteria to help you differentiate between healthy, productive deep thinking and destructive overthinking:

1. The Outcome: Clarity vs. Confusion

- **Deep Thinking:** Leads to greater clarity and understanding. You feel confident in your decision-making and more informed about your choices.

- **Overthinking:** Creates confusion and self-doubt. The more you think, the less certain you feel, often leading to second-guessing and indecision.

A person considering a career change might engage in deep thinking by researching options, assessing their skills, and making a pros-and-cons list. This reflection helps them gain clarity on the best path forward. In contrast, overthinking might involve constantly worrying about every possible risk and imagining worst-case scenarios, leaving them too paralyzed to make a decision.

2. The Emotional Response: Calm vs. Anxiety

- **Deep Thinking:** Feels calm, purposeful, and focused. It's driven by curiosity and a desire to gain insights.

- **Overthinking:** Feels frantic, anxious, and overwhelming. It's driven by fear, self-doubt, and the need for control.

Planning a big event, such as a wedding, can involve deep thinking about logistics and guest preferences. If done calmly, this planning is enjoyable and productive. However, if the planning turns into constant worry about things going wrong, it becomes overthinking, causing stress and anxiety.

3. The Focus: Solutions vs. Problems

- **Deep Thinking:** Is solution-oriented. You focus on finding answers and making progress.

- **Overthinking:** Is problem-focused. You dwell on issues, replay scenarios in your head, and get stuck in a loop of "what ifs."

When faced with a conflict at work, deep thinking might involve considering different approaches to resolve the issue and improve communication. Overthinking, on the other hand, might involve obsessing over what was said, fearing the worst possible outcomes, and ruminating without taking action.

Checklist: Are You Overthinking or Deep Thinking?
Use this checklist to identify when your thinking is shifting from deep reflection to unproductive rumination:

1. **Do you feel more confused the longer you think about it?**

   - If yes, you're likely overthinking.

2. **Are you focusing on solutions or just replaying problems?**

   - If you're stuck on problems, you're likely overthinking.

3. **Do you feel calm and curious, or anxious and overwhelmed?**

   - If anxiety is taking over, it's a sign of overthinking.

4. **Are you using your thinking time to gain clarity or to avoid taking action?**

- Avoidance is a key indicator of overthinking.

When you notice yourself overthinking, take a moment to pause and shift your focus. Ask yourself, "What's one small action I can take right now to move forward?" This helps break the cycle of rumination and puts you back on the path of productive thinking.

When Thinking Turns into Overthinking

Overthinking is when our thought process becomes excessive and repetitive, causing us to dwell on problems or situations without making progress. Unlike productive thinking, which aims for clarity, overthinking leads to confusion and often makes us feel stuck. It can manifest in various ways, such as replaying past conversations, second-guessing every decision, or worrying about worst-case scenarios that may never happen.

Jesus addressed the issue of excessive worry in Matthew 6:27 (NIV): *"Can any one of you by worrying add a single hour to your life?"* This rhetorical question illustrates that overthinking and worrying do not contribute to solving our problems; instead, they waste our time and energy.

Imagine a person who is preparing to give a presentation at work. Instead of focusing on refining their slides and practicing their speech, they start overthinking every detail—worrying about what the audience might think, fearing they might forget a point, or doubting the quality of their content. As a result, they become paralyzed by fear and are unable to complete their preparation effectively.

Common Causes of Overthinking

Overthinking often stems from specific triggers or underlying issues, such as:

1. **Fear of Failure:**

   Many people overthink because they are afraid of making mistakes. They believe that if they analyze every detail, they can avoid failure. However, this mindset often leads to procrastination and inaction. Ecclesiastes 11:4 (NIV) warns, *"Whoever watches the wind will not plant; whoever looks at the clouds will not reap."*

The fear of potential failure can prevent us from taking the necessary steps toward success.

2. **Stress and Anxiety:**

   Stressful situations can trigger a cycle of overthinking, especially when we feel overwhelmed or uncertain. The mind races with 'what if' scenarios, amplifying the stress rather than alleviating it. This kind of rumination can lead to heightened anxiety and a sense of losing control.

3. **Perfectionism:**

   Perfectionists tend to overthink because they are constantly striving for flawlessness. They may revise their work endlessly or delay starting tasks due to the fear of producing anything less than perfect. This pursuit of perfection can become paralyzing, preventing them from ever finishing what they start.

An artist who is a perfectionist might spend hours reworking a single painting, never feeling satisfied with the result. Instead of moving on to the next piece, they become stuck, unable to complete the artwork. This cycle of overthinking hampers their creativity and productivity.

The Concept of "Analysis Paralysis"

Analysis paralysis is a state where overthinking prevents us from making any decisions or taking action. It occurs when we become so caught up in analyzing every possible outcome that we fail to choose a path forward. This concept is particularly relevant in our modern world, where the abundance of information and options can overwhelm us.

In James 1:8 (NIV), it says, "*Such a person is double-minded and unstable in all they do.*" This verse captures the essence of analysis paralysis, where indecision leads to instability and inaction. A double-minded person is torn between choices, unable to commit to one and move forward.

A person shopping for a new smartphone might spend weeks comparing different models, reading reviews, and analyzing every feature. They become so engrossed in the process that they cannot decide which phone to buy. This delay is not due to a lack of information but rather an excess of it, leading to decision fatigue.

Overcoming Analysis Paralysis

The key to overcoming analysis paralysis is to set clear criteria for decision-making and limit the amount of time spent on analysis. It's important to remind ourselves that no decision is perfect, and that taking action is often better than remaining stuck in indecision.

Practical Tips:

- Set a deadline for making decisions and stick to it.

- Simplify your options by narrowing them down to a few key choices.

- Trust your instincts and remember that mistakes are part of the learning process.

Understanding the difference between healthy thinking and overthinking is crucial for personal growth and success. While thoughtful reflection is a valuable skill that can lead to insight and clarity, overthinking can trap us in a loop of worry and doubt.

By recognizing the signs of overthinking and addressing its causes, we can break free from the cycle and move towards a more balanced and productive mindset.

CHAPTER 2: THE CONSEQUENCES OF OVERTHINKING

The Burden of Overthinking

Overthinking is often described as a thief of joy. It burdens the mind, clouds our judgment, and leaves us feeling emotionally exhausted. The quote, "The heaviest burdens that we carry are the thoughts in our head," captures this reality perfectly. When we get trapped in a loop of constant rumination, we carry a weight that is invisible to others but feels unbearably heavy to us. These thoughts can revolve around regrets from the past, worries about the future, or doubts about our current choices, creating a mental load that can be overwhelming.

In Proverbs 12:25 (NIV), it says, *"Anxiety weighs down the heart, but a kind word cheers it up."* This verse highlights how the burden of anxious thoughts can weigh us down emotionally, affecting our mood and overall well-being. Overthinking keeps us focused on negative possibilities, draining our emotional energy and making it difficult to experience peace and contentment.

Consider a person who made a mistake at work. Instead of acknowledging it and moving on, they replay the scenario over and over in their mind, thinking about what they should have done differently. This self-inflicted emotional turmoil doesn't change the past; it only increases their anxiety and stress, making it harder to focus on future tasks.

Overthinking Disconnects Us from Reality

One of the most damaging aspects of overthinking is that it pulls us away from the present moment. When we are trapped in our thoughts, we become disconnected from reality and the world around us. We might find ourselves so engrossed in our worries that we miss out on important opportunities or fail to appreciate what is happening right now.

Matthew 6:34 (NIV) advises, "*Therefore do not worry about tomorrow, for tomorrow will worry about itself. Each day has enough trouble of its own.*" This verse encourages us to focus on the present rather than getting lost in concerns about the future. Overthinking makes us live in a hypothetical world of 'what ifs' rather than experiencing life as it unfolds.

Imagine someone at a family gathering; instead of enjoying the moment, they are preoccupied with worries about work or future problems. They miss out on creating meaningful memories because they are mentally absent, disconnected from the joy and connection happening around them.

To combat the disconnect caused by overthinking, practice mindfulness. Engage in activities that anchor you to the present, such as deep breathing exercises, meditation, or even simply noticing the sights and sounds around you. Mindfulness helps bring your focus back to reality, easing the burden of excessive thoughts.

Overthinking and Mental Health

Overthinking is closely linked to mental health issues such as anxiety and depression. When our minds are constantly fixated on negative thoughts, it can create a cycle of worry and fear that fuels anxiety. Similarly, ruminating over past mistakes or negative experiences can lead to feelings of sadness and hopelessness, which are common symptoms of depression.

Philippians 4:6-7 (NIV) offers comforting guidance: "*Do not be anxious about anything, but in every situation, by prayer and petition, with thanksgiving, present your requests to God. And the peace of God, which transcends all understanding, will guard your hearts and your minds in Christ Jesus.*" This scripture emphasizes the importance of turning our worries over to God and trusting in His peace rather than allowing our minds to be consumed by fear.

Consider a person who frequently overthinks social interactions. They may replay conversations in their head, worrying that they said the wrong thing or offended someone unintentionally. This type of rumination can lead to social anxiety, where the fear of making a mistake becomes so overwhelming that they start avoiding social situations altogether. The cycle of overthinking reinforces the anxiety, making it difficult to break free.

To better understand why overthinking often leads to anxiety, let's take a look at what happens in the brain during periods of excessive worry.

Understanding the Role of the Amygdala

The amygdala is a small, almond-shaped structure in the brain that plays a key role in our emotional responses, especially fear and anxiety. It is part of the brain's limbic system, which is responsible for processing emotions and reacting to threats. When we encounter a stressful situation or start overthinking a potential problem, the amygdala becomes activated, triggering the body's fight-or-flight response.

Overthinking often causes a cascade of negative thoughts, which the amygdala interprets as a sign of danger. Even if the perceived threat is purely hypothetical (e.g., worrying about an upcoming presentation or replaying a past mistake), the amygdala responds as though the threat is real. This triggers the release of stress hormones like cortisol and adrenaline, leading to physical symptoms such as a racing heart, sweaty palms, and shallow breathing.

Imagine you are lying in bed, replaying a conversation you had earlier in the day, worrying that you might have said something wrong. As you continue to ruminate, your amygdala kicks into high gear, sending signals to your body that there is a threat. Even though the threat is not immediate or physical, your body reacts as though it is, making it difficult to relax or fall asleep.

Practical Techniques to Calm the Amygdala and Reduce Anxiety

Understanding the brain's role in overthinking can help us develop strategies to calm the mind and interrupt the anxiety response. Here are some practical techniques:

1. Mindful Breathing:

Deep, slow breathing activates the parasympathetic nervous system, which helps counteract the fight-or-flight response triggered by the amygdala. Practice inhaling slowly through your nose for a count of four, holding your breath for four counts, and then exhaling through your mouth for four counts. Repeat this several times to calm your nervous system.

Psalm 46:10 (NIV) says, *"Be still, and know that I am God."* This verse encourages us to pause and find calmness, reminding us to trust in God's control instead of letting anxiety overwhelm us.

2. Grounding Exercises:

Grounding techniques help you focus on the present moment, reducing the power of anxious thoughts. One effective method is the "5-4-3-2-1" exercise:

- Name 5 things you can see.
- Name 4 things you can touch.
- Name 3 things you can hear.
- Name 2 things you can smell.
- Name 1 thing you can taste.

By focusing on your senses, you shift your attention away from the racing thoughts and give your amygdala a chance to calm down.

3. Reframing Anxious Thoughts:

When the amygdala triggers anxiety, it's often because we are interpreting a situation as more dangerous or threatening than it actually is. Take a moment to ask yourself, "Is this thought based on fact, or am I imagining the worst-case scenario?" Reframe your thoughts with a more balanced perspective, reminding yourself that not every negative thought is a true reflection of reality.

If you're worried about failing a job interview, instead of thinking, "I'm going to mess this up," reframe it to, "I've prepared well, and I'll do my best. Even if I don't get this job, it's an opportunity to learn and grow."

Practice these techniques regularly, even when you're not feeling anxious. By training your brain to respond differently to stress, you can reduce the impact of the amygdala's fight-or-flight response and build a more resilient mindset.

Understanding the role of the amygdala in triggering anxiety helps us see that overthinking is not just a mental habit—it's a physiological response. By learning how to calm the mind and manage this response, we can break free from the cycle of anxiety and regain control over our thoughts. Remember, God's peace is available to us when we choose to trust Him instead of succumbing to fear. Philippians 4:7 (NIV) promises, *"And the peace of God, which transcends all understanding, will guard your hearts and your minds in Christ Jesus."*

The Cycle of Self-Doubt and Inaction

Overthinking often triggers a cycle of self-doubt, which leads to hesitation and, eventually, inaction. When we overanalyze every detail of a situation, we become paralyzed by the fear of making a wrong decision. This phenomenon is known as analysis paralysis, where the sheer amount of thinking prevents us from taking any meaningful steps forward.

James 1:6-8 (NIV) speaks to the instability that comes from being filled with doubt: *"But when you ask, you must believe and not doubt, because the one who doubts is like a wave of the sea, blown and tossed by the wind. That person should not expect to receive anything from the Lord. Such a person is double-minded and unstable in all they do."* This passage highlights how self-doubt can create instability in our lives, preventing us from moving forward with confidence and trust.

A young entrepreneur has a promising idea for a new business venture. However, instead of acting on their plan, they start overthinking every aspect of the business: the potential risks, the competition, the possibility of failure. As their doubts grow, they hesitate to take the first step, and eventually, the idea remains just that—an idea. The opportunity is lost, not because it wasn't viable, but because the fear of failure led to inaction.

Breaking the Cycle of Overthinking

To break free from the cycle of overthinking and self-doubt, we must learn to take action despite our fears. This involves embracing a growth mindset, where mistakes are seen as opportunities to learn rather than as signs of failure. In 2 Timothy 1:7 (NIV), we are reminded, *"For the Spirit God gave us does not make us timid, but gives us power, love, and self-discipline."* This verse encourages us to replace fear and doubt with courage and self-discipline, empowering us to make decisions and move forward.

Practical Tips:

- Practice self-compassion by treating yourself with the same kindness and understanding you would offer a friend.

- Limit the time you spend analyzing a decision. Set a time limit, make your choice, and move forward.

- Focus on progress, not perfection. Accept that mistakes are a part of life and an essential component of growth.

The consequences of overthinking can be severe, affecting not only our emotional well-being but also our mental health and ability to take action. By understanding the burden of overthinking and recognizing its impact, we can begin to challenge our thought patterns and make changes that lead to a healthier, more balanced mindset. Remember, while thinking is an essential part of our decision-making process, it should be a tool for clarity, not a source of endless doubt and worry.

~ 44 ~

CHAPTER 3: EMBRACING INDIVIDUAL STRENGTHS

The Beauty of Our Uniqueness

Each of us is uniquely crafted with a set of strengths, weaknesses, interests, and passions. This diversity is not accidental; it reflects the vast creative nature of God. As Psalm 139:14 (NIV) says, "*I praise you because I am fearfully and wonderfully made; your works are wonderful, I know that full well.*" Our individual qualities and differences are what make us valuable and enable us to contribute in various ways to our families, communities, and the world.

Embracing our uniqueness involves recognizing that our strengths are gifts we can use to serve others, while our weaknesses are opportunities for growth and collaboration. We don't need to be good at everything, but we can excel when we focus on our areas of strength and passion. Instead of comparing ourselves to others, we should celebrate our distinctiveness and trust that each of us has a specific role to play.

Consider the differences between an artist and an engineer. The artist might excel in creativity and emotional expression, creating beautiful works that inspire others. On the other hand, the engineer might have a talent for problem-solving and logical thinking, developing innovative solutions to complex issues. Both roles are valuable and necessary, even though they require completely different skill sets.

The diversity of thought and action is what drives progress and innovation. When we embrace our unique perspectives and talents, we bring a variety of ideas and approaches to the table, leading to better outcomes. Romans 12:6 (NIV) states, *"We have different gifts, according to the grace given to each of us."* This scripture reminds us that our diverse gifts are intentional and that working together with our unique strengths enriches the collective whole.

In a corporate setting, a diverse team of individuals can achieve remarkable success by leveraging their different skills and experiences. While one person might be a strategic thinker who excels at planning, another might be action-oriented and skilled at execution. By combining these strengths, the team can develop a comprehensive strategy and implement it effectively, achieving their goals more efficiently.

To make the most of your unique strengths, take time to identify your natural talents and passions. Reflect on what activities make you feel energized and fulfilled. Focus on developing these areas and don't be discouraged by your weaknesses. Instead, find ways to collaborate with others whose strengths complement your own.

Embracing our individual strengths is the first step, but developing self-trust is essential to avoid falling into the trap of overthinking and self-doubt.

Building Self-Trust: The Key to Overcoming Overthinking

One of the primary reasons people fall into the cycle of overthinking is a lack of self-trust. When we don't fully trust our own judgment, we tend to second-guess every decision, replay scenarios in our minds, and seek endless reassurance from others. Building self-trust is a powerful antidote to this habit because it helps us develop confidence in our choices, allowing us to take decisive action without being paralyzed by doubt.

A practical way to start building self-trust is by keeping small promises to yourself. These are simple commitments that you make and follow through on consistently. It might be something as small as setting a goal to wake up 10 minutes earlier each day, drinking a glass of water every morning, or completing a daily task on your to-do list.

Imagine you promise yourself that you'll exercise for 10 minutes each day. By honoring this commitment, you send a message to your subconscious mind that you can be trusted to follow through. Over time, these small wins build a foundation of trust, making it easier for you to rely on your own decisions in larger, more complex situations.

In Proverbs 3:5-6 (NIV), it says, "*Trust in the Lord with all your heart and lean not on your own understanding; in all your ways submit to him, and he will make your paths straight.*" While this verse emphasizes trusting God's guidance, it also implies that our actions should reflect our faith. By making small commitments and keeping them, we practice a form of self-trust that aligns with our faith in God's direction.

Strategies for Developing Self-Trust

Here are some actionable steps you can take to build self-trust and reduce overthinking:

1. Start with Small, Achievable Goals:

Set a goal that is realistic and achievable, no matter how small it may seem. Follow through consistently to prove to yourself that you can be trusted to take action.

If you find it hard to trust your ability to make decisions, start with small daily choices. Decide what you'll have for breakfast the night before and stick to your decision. This exercise might seem trivial, but it trains your brain to trust your initial choices.

2. Practice Self-Affirmations:

Affirmations are positive statements that reinforce your trust in yourself. By regularly repeating affirmations, you rewire your brain to believe in your capabilities.

Example Affirmations:

- "I trust myself to make wise decisions."
- "I am capable of handling whatever comes my way."
- "Every choice I make is a step towards growth."

3. Reflect on Past Successes:

Take time to reflect on moments in your life when you made good decisions or handled challenges successfully. Remind yourself of these instances to reinforce your belief in your own abilities.

Keep a journal where you note past achievements, even small ones. On days when you struggle with self-doubt, revisit these entries to remind yourself of what you've accomplished and the good decisions you've made.

How Self-Trust Reduces the Tendency to Overthink

When you trust yourself, you no longer feel the need to seek endless reassurance or analyze every decision from multiple angles. You become more comfortable with uncertainty because you have confidence in your ability to handle whatever outcome that may arise. This shift in mindset reduces the mental burden of overthinking and allows you to move forward with clarity and purpose.

A person preparing for a public speaking event might usually overthink their speech, worrying about how the audience will react. However, if they have built self-trust through consistent practice and positive self-affirmation, they can approach the event with confidence, trusting their preparation and instincts.

Each time you make a decision, big or small, pause and acknowledge it. Say to yourself, "I trust this decision and will stand by it." This simple practice reinforces the habit of self-trust and reduces the urge to second-guess yourself.

Building self-trust is a gradual process, but it is one of the most powerful ways to combat overthinking. By keeping small promises to yourself, using positive affirmations, and reflecting on your past successes, you can develop the confidence needed to make decisions without hesitation. Remember, self-trust is not about being infallible—it's about believing in your ability to handle whatever comes your way, trusting in both yourself and God's guidance. Isaiah 26:3 (NIV) reassures us: *"You will keep in perfect peace those whose minds are steadfast, because they trust in you."*

Case Studies: The Thinker and the Doer

Albert Einstein: The Power of Deep Contemplation

Albert Einstein is widely regarded as one of the greatest thinkers of all time. His ability to dive deep into complex ideas and theories transformed our understanding of physics. Einstein's theory of relativity, for example, changed the way we perceive time and space. He once said, *"Imagination is more important than knowledge. For knowledge is limited, whereas imagination embraces the entire world."*

Einstein's success was rooted in his capacity for deep contemplation. He wasn't afraid to spend long periods of time pondering abstract concepts and exploring the unknown. This type of deep thinking allowed him to make groundbreaking discoveries that others couldn't see. However, what made Einstein truly remarkable was his ability to take these theoretical ideas and apply them in practical ways, balancing thought with action.

Einstein's famous thought experiment about a person riding alongside a beam of light led him to develop the theory of special relativity. He used his imagination to explore possibilities beyond what could be tested at the time, yet he also grounded his theories in scientific principles and experimentation, leading to real-world applications like GPS technology.

While deep thinking can lead to significant breakthroughs, it must be balanced with practical action. In James 2:17 (NIV), it says, "*In the same way, faith by itself, if it is not accompanied by action, is dead.*" This verse emphasizes the importance of not only having ideas and insights but also acting upon them. Einstein understood this balance; his theories were not just intellectual exercises but tools that expanded our technological capabilities and improved our understanding of the universe.

Embrace time for deep thinking and reflection, but also set deadlines and take steps to test your ideas in the real world. This balance will help you move from merely thinking about possibilities to creating tangible results.

Lionel Messi: The Genius of Spontaneous Action

Lionel Messi is a world-renowned footballer known for his incredible talent, quick decision-making, and instinctive play on the field. Messi's genius lies not only in his physical abilities but also in his capacity to read the game and react almost instantaneously. Unlike Einstein's deep, contemplative approach, Messi's success comes from his ability to make split-second decisions based on instinct and intuition.

Messi's approach highlights the value of spontaneous action. He doesn't get bogged down by overanalyzing every move; instead, he trusts his instincts and years of practice. This ability to act decisively is what makes him one of the greatest footballers of all time. In 1 Corinthians 9:24 (NIV), Paul writes, *"Do you not know that in a race all the runners run, but only one gets the prize? Run in such a way as to get the prize.*" This verse speaks to the importance of being decisive and giving your best effort in every situation.

During a critical match, Messi often finds himself surrounded by defenders with little time to think. Instead of hesitating, he relies on his instinctive play and years of practice to make a move that leaves the defenders behind. His spontaneous actions often lead to spectacular goals, showcasing the power of trusting your instincts and taking immediate action.

Messi's approach also underscores the importance of balancing instinctive action with thoughtful strategy. While he relies heavily on his natural instincts, those instincts are honed through countless hours of practice and preparation. Messi's success is not accidental; it's the result of disciplined training combined with the ability to act decisively in the moment.

Trust your instincts, especially in situations where quick decisions are required. However, make sure to develop and refine your skills through consistent practice and preparation. This way, when the moment comes to act, you can do so with confidence and precision.

The case studies of Albert Einstein and Lionel Messi illustrate two different approaches to success: deep contemplation and spontaneous action. Both methods have their merits, but the key lies in finding a balance that suits your unique strengths. Whether you are a thinker like Einstein or a doer like Messi, embrace your individuality and use it to your advantage. As you learn to balance thoughtful reflection with decisive action, you will unlock your full potential and make meaningful contributions to the world around you.

CHAPTER 4: THE THIN LINE BETWEEN PERFECTIONISM AND PROGRESS

Creativity is a powerful gift, allowing us to express ourselves, solve problems, and innovate in unique ways. It thrives on inspiration, imagination, and the willingness to explore the unknown. However, for many creative individuals, the same mind that generates brilliant ideas can also become a source of overthinking. When we start overanalyzing every detail of our work, we risk falling into a trap where creativity is stifled by self-doubt and fear.

Vincent van Gogh, one of the most famous and influential artists in history, often struggled with perfectionism and self-doubt. Despite his incredible talent, van Gogh was known to obsess over his paintings, frequently doubting their quality and significance. He once said, "If you hear a voice within you say, 'You cannot paint,' then by all means paint, and that voice will be silenced." This quote reflects the inner battle he faced—an artist torn between inspiration and self-criticism.

Van Gogh's tendency to overthink often led him to question his creative choices, making it difficult for him to appreciate his own work. He constantly revised his paintings, seeking an unattainable standard of perfection. While his deep contemplation allowed him to create masterpieces, it also contributed to his emotional turmoil and self-imposed pressure.

Balancing Inspiration and Self-Doubt

Inspiration and self-doubt often exist in a delicate balance. While inspiration drives us to create and explore new ideas, self-doubt can either serve as a motivator for improvement or become a barrier to creativity. The key is to recognize when self-doubt begins to overshadow inspiration and leads to overthinking. Proverbs 16:3 (NIV) provides a helpful perspective: "*Commit to the Lord whatever you do, and he will establish your plans.*" This verse reminds us that we should trust our creative process and commit our efforts to a higher purpose, rather than allowing fear and doubt to dictate our actions.

A writer working on a novel might start with a burst of inspiration, excited to bring their story to life. However, as they progress, they begin second-guessing their plot choices, worrying about potential flaws, and revising endlessly. This overthinking can lead to a creative block, where the writer feels unable to move forward. Instead of letting inspiration flow, they become trapped by their own self-criticism.

To avoid falling into the trap of overthinking, set boundaries for your creative process. Give yourself permission to create imperfectly and embrace the idea that your first draft or initial work is just the beginning. Focus on expressing your ideas without judging them too harshly, knowing that there will be time later for refinement.

Perfectionism: The Enemy of Progress

Perfectionism is often seen as a positive trait, associated with high standards and a strong work ethic. However, striving for perfection can become a significant barrier to progress. When we aim for flawlessness in everything we do, we set ourselves up for disappointment and frustration, as perfection is an unrealistic and unattainable goal. This mindset can lead to procrastination, where we delay starting or completing tasks because we fear they won't be perfect.

Ecclesiastes 11:4 (NIV) speaks to this issue: *"Whoever watches the wind will not plant; whoever looks at the clouds will not reap."* This verse illustrates how perfectionism can cause inaction—when we wait for the perfect conditions or the perfect result, we miss the opportunity to take meaningful steps forward.

A student working on a school project may spend hours trying to perfect every detail before submitting it. They revise their work repeatedly, never feeling satisfied with the outcome. As a result, they might submit the project late or avoid completing it altogether, fearing it won't meet their own impossible standards. In the end, their desire for perfection hinders their progress and affects their performance.

The Procrastination-Perfectionism Loop

Perfectionism often leads to a vicious cycle of procrastination and stagnation. The fear of making mistakes or producing less-than-perfect work causes us to delay taking action. We might tell ourselves that we're just "waiting for the right moment" or "still working on it," but in reality, we're stuck in a loop where nothing gets done. Over time, this stagnation erodes our confidence and makes it even harder to start new projects.

James 4:17 (NIV) offers a sobering reminder: *"If anyone, then, knows the good they ought to do and doesn't do it, it is sin for them."* This verse highlights the importance of taking action rather than delaying due to fear or perfectionism. By focusing too much on perfecting every detail, we risk neglecting the good that can come from simply starting and completing a task.

Consider a budding entrepreneur with a great business idea. They spend months refining their business plan, perfecting their pitch, and tweaking their product. However, they never feel ready to launch, constantly fearing that something isn't quite right. This delay prevents them from entering the market, allowing competitors to gain an advantage. Instead of making progress and learning from their experiences, they remain stuck in a cycle of over-preparation.

Accepting Imperfection as Part of Growth

The path to growth and creativity is paved with mistakes and imperfections. Rather than viewing these as failures, we should see them as valuable learning experiences. When we accept that imperfection is a natural part of the creative process, we open ourselves up to experimentation, discovery, and progress. 2 Corinthians 12:9 (NIV) says, *"But he said to me, 'My grace is sufficient for you, for my power is made perfect in weakness.'"* This scripture encourages us to embrace our imperfections and trust that God's strength can shine through our weaknesses.

Practical Tips for Overcoming Perfectionism:

1. **Set Realistic Goals:** Aim for progress, not perfection. Focus on completing tasks rather than making them flawless.

2. **Adopt a Growth Mindset:** View mistakes as opportunities to learn and grow. Celebrate your efforts, even if the results aren't perfect.

3. **Practice Self-Compassion:** Be kind to yourself when things don't go as planned. Remember that everyone makes mistakes, and it's part of the journey.

There is a fine line between striving for excellence and being trapped by perfectionism. Creativity thrives when we give ourselves the freedom to explore and experiment, free from the fear of making mistakes. By embracing imperfection as a part of the creative process, we can move forward with confidence and make meaningful progress. Remember, it is better to complete something imperfectly than to leave it unfinished in pursuit of perfection. As we let go of our need for flawlessness, we open the door to growth, innovation, and the true expression of our creative potential.

When faced with the urge to be perfect, our first instinct is often to suppress any negative or anxious thoughts. However, this approach can backfire, causing even more distress. Instead, we can learn to replace these thoughts with positive imagery and affirmations.

Replacing Negative Thoughts Instead of Suppressing Them

Perfectionism often goes hand in hand with a flood of negative, self-critical thoughts. The natural response is to try to push these thoughts away or suppress them, hoping they will disappear. However, research shows that attempting to suppress negative thoughts often has the opposite effect—it makes them stronger. This phenomenon is known as the "rebound effect," where the more we try not to think about something, the more it dominates our mind.

Imagine you tell yourself, "Don't think about making a mistake during the presentation." The harder you try not to think about it, the more vivid and persistent the thought becomes. This mental struggle adds to your stress and increases the likelihood of overthinking.

Instead of suppressing negative thoughts, try replacing them with positive, empowering imagery or affirmations. This technique works because it redirects your focus and changes the narrative in your mind. Rather than fighting against the negative thought, you introduce a new, positive thought that aligns with your goals and intentions.

If you find yourself thinking, "I'm never going to get this right," replace it with, "I am learning and improving with each step." Instead of saying, "I always mess up," reframe it to, "I've overcome challenges before, and I can handle this too."

Practical Strategy: The Thought Replacement Exercise

Here's a simple exercise to help you practice replacing negative thoughts:

1. **Identify the Negative Thought:**

   Pay attention to your inner dialogue and notice when a negative thought arises. Acknowledge it without judgment.

   Example:

   "I'm not good enough to complete this project."

2. **Pause and Reframe:**

   Instead of suppressing the thought, pause and consciously choose a new, positive thought to replace it. Use an affirmation or a visualization of a positive outcome.

   Example:

   Replace "I'm not good enough" with "I am capable and equipped to handle this task. I have the skills I need."

3. **Visualize Success:**

   Close your eyes and take a moment to visualize yourself successfully completing the task. Imagine the feeling of accomplishment and pride that comes with it.

Example:

Picture yourself confidently presenting your ideas in a meeting or crossing the finish line of a race you've trained for. This positive imagery shifts your focus away from fear and towards possibility.

Philippians 4:8 (NIV) advises us, *"Finally, brothers and sisters, whatever is true, whatever is noble, whatever is right, whatever is pure, whatever is lovely, whatever is admirable—if anything is excellent or praiseworthy—think about such things."* This verse encourages us to focus on uplifting and positive thoughts, rather than allowing negative thinking to take root in our minds.

Why This Technique Works

Replacing negative thoughts is effective because it interrupts the cycle of self-criticism that fuels perfectionism. It allows you to break free from the pattern of rumination and creates a space for more constructive and supportive thinking. When you practice this consistently, you start to rewire your brain, making it easier to default to positive thoughts rather than falling back into the habit of negative self-talk.

A student preparing for an important exam might worry, "I'm going to fail this test." Instead of trying to suppress this thought, they can replace it with, "I've studied hard, and I'm well-prepared. I'm ready to do my best." This shift in thinking reduces anxiety and helps the student approach the exam with a more confident mindset.

When you notice yourself getting caught in a perfectionist thought loop, take a moment to practice this replacement technique. Write down the negative thought, then write a positive affirmation or visualization next to it. Read it out loud and focus on the positive statement. Over time, this habit will help you transform your inner dialogue.

Replacing negative thoughts with positive ones is a powerful tool in overcoming the grip of perfectionism. By redirecting your focus, you can break free from the cycle of self-doubt and anxiety that holds you back. Remember, God's word reminds us to think about what is true, noble, and praiseworthy. Trust that with each positive thought you choose, you are aligning yourself with His truth and moving closer to a mindset of growth and progress.

CHAPTER 5: FINDING BALANCE

The Power of Action Over Perfect Planning

Many people fall into the trap of waiting for the "perfect moment" before taking action, believing that they need the ideal plan or the right conditions to proceed. However, the reality is that perfection is an illusion, and waiting for the perfect time often leads to inaction. In Ecclesiastes 11:4 (NIV), it says, "*Whoever watches the wind will not plant; whoever looks at the clouds will not reap.*" This verse illustrates the danger of hesitating and overanalyzing instead of taking the necessary steps forward. Life's opportunities rarely present themselves under flawless conditions, and if we keep waiting, we might miss them entirely.

Taking action, even when the situation is less than ideal, can lead to unexpected progress and growth. The key is to start with what you have, where you are, and make improvements along the way. By moving forward, we gain momentum and create a path to success.

Consider a person who dreams of starting a new business. They spend years planning, researching, and waiting for the "perfect" economic climate. Meanwhile, competitors who took action sooner have already established themselves in the market. The difference is not necessarily in the quality of the plans but in the willingness to take the first step, learn from experiences, and adapt.

One of the most effective ways to overcome the tendency to over-plan and procrastinate is to set clear deadlines and break tasks into small, actionable steps. Deadlines create a sense of urgency, helping us move from thinking to doing. Breaking down a project into manageable parts makes it less overwhelming and allows us to make steady progress.

In James 4:13-15 (NIV), it says, "*Now listen, you who say, 'Today or tomorrow we will go to this or that city, spend a year there, carry on business and make money.' Why, you do not even know what will happen tomorrow.*" This scripture reminds us that we cannot predict the future, so it's better to take action now rather than delay indefinitely.

A student preparing for a final exam might feel overwhelmed by the volume of materials they need to study. Instead of trying to learn everything at once, they can break their study plan into small, focused sessions, covering one topic at a time. By setting a schedule and sticking to it, they make consistent progress, reducing stress and increasing their chances of success.

Practical Tips for Taking Action:

1. **Set a Start Date:** Decide when you will begin your project or task and hold yourself accountable.

2. **Break It Down:** Divide your goal into smaller, specific tasks that can be completed in a short period.

3. **Take the First Step:** Commit to taking one small action today, even if it feels insignificant. The momentum will build as you continue.

While taking action is vital, there are times when deep thinking and careful analysis are necessary. Let's explore when overthinking can actually be useful, and when it becomes a hindrance to progress.

Scenarios Where Overthinking Is Useful vs. When It's Not

Overthinking often gets a bad reputation, but there are times when deep, reflective thinking can be incredibly valuable. The key lies in recognizing when this kind of analysis is helpful and when it starts to hinder progress. Here's a guide to help you differentiate between scenarios where deep thinking is beneficial and when it becomes detrimental:

When Overthinking (Deep Thinking) Is Beneficial

1. **Strategic Planning and Long-Term Decisions**

   Deep thinking is essential when making strategic plans or long-term decisions that have significant consequences. This includes scenarios like planning a business expansion, choosing a career path, or making a major financial investment. In these cases, careful analysis and consideration of all possible outcomes can help you make a more informed decision.

Before launching a new product, a business leader might spend weeks or even months analyzing market trends, customer needs, and potential risks. This level of deep thinking helps to ensure that the product meets the market demand and minimizes the risk of failure.

2. **Complex Problem Solving**

When faced with a complex problem that requires a thorough understanding of multiple factors, deep thinking can be highly effective. It allows you to explore different solutions, consider various perspectives, and weigh the pros and cons.

An engineer designing a new system might engage in deep thinking to anticipate potential issues, analyze different design options, and find the most efficient solution. In this scenario, taking the time to think deeply can prevent costly mistakes.

3. Analyzing Past Mistakes for Growth

Reflecting deeply on past experiences and mistakes can be beneficial when done constructively. It helps you learn from what went wrong, understand what could have been done differently, and apply those lessons to future situations.

After a failed project, a manager might conduct a detailed review of what went wrong. By analyzing the mistakes made, they can identify areas for improvement and create a more effective strategy for the next project.

Proverbs 21:5 (NIV) says, "*The plans of the diligent lead to profit as surely as haste leads to poverty.*" This verse emphasizes the value of careful planning and deep thought, suggesting that taking time to think things through can lead to greater success.

When Overthinking Becomes Detrimental

1. **Daily Decision-Making and Routine Tasks**

   Overthinking everyday decisions, such as what to wear or what to eat, can waste time and drain mental energy. These types of choices do not require extensive analysis and overthinking them often leads to indecision and stress.

   A person might spend 20 minutes debating whether to send an email now or later, replaying possible scenarios in their mind. This kind of overthinking is unproductive and prevents them from moving on to more important tasks.

2. **Taking Action on New Opportunities**

   When a new opportunity presents itself, excessive analysis can lead to missed chances. While it's important to consider the risks, spending too much time overthinking the potential downsides can result in paralysis, causing you to miss out on valuable experiences.

   Someone might be offered a chance to join a new project at work but spends so much time worrying about whether they're fully prepared that they miss the opportunity to say yes. By the time they decide, the project has already been assigned to someone else.

3. **Handling Social Interactions and Conversations**

Overthinking past conversations or social interactions often leads to unnecessary stress. When you replay a conversation repeatedly, wondering if you said the wrong thing, you create anxiety that serves no productive purpose.

After attending a party, a person might spend hours replaying a conversation they had, worrying about whether they sounded awkward. This type of rumination doesn't change the outcome and only increases social anxiety, making it harder to enjoy future interactions.

Ask yourself, "Is this decision critical to my long-term goals, or is it something I can decide quickly and move on from?" If the choice is minor or can be easily adjusted later, it's better to act swiftly rather than overthink it.

Finding the Right Balance

Understanding when to engage in deep thinking and when to take swift action is key to finding balance. If the decision involves a long-term commitment, complex problem, or significant risk, then deep thinking can be beneficial. However, if the decision is minor or time-sensitive, it's better to act quickly and adjust as needed.

A writer working on a novel might spend weeks developing the plot (deep thinking), but when it comes to writing the first draft, they should focus on getting words on the page rather than overthinking every sentence. The initial draft can always be revised later.

Ecclesiastes 3:1 (NIV) reminds us, "*There is a time for everything, and a season for every activity under the heavens.*" This verse speaks to the importance of recognizing when it's time to reflect and when it's time to act.

Deep thinking can be a valuable asset when used appropriately, but it becomes a hindrance when it leads to indecision and stress. By understanding the difference between scenarios that require thoughtful reflection and those that call for quick action, you can make better decisions and move forward with confidence. Remember, it's about finding the right balance—embracing both reflection and action to live a more purposeful life.

Learning from Mistakes and Adjusting as You Go

One of the biggest obstacles to taking action is the fear of making mistakes. Many people hesitate to move forward because they are afraid of failure or of looking foolish. However, mistakes are an inevitable part of the journey toward success. They are not indicators of incompetence but rather opportunities for growth and improvement. In Proverbs 24:16 (NIV), it says, *"For though the righteous fall seven times, they rise again."* This verse encourages us to get back up after a fall, understanding that setbacks are part of the process.

The most successful people in history are not those who never made mistakes, but those who learned from them and used those lessons to refine their approach. Thomas Edison, for example, famously said, "I have not failed. I've just found 10,000 ways that won't work." His perseverance and willingness to learn from his mistakes led to the invention of the light bulb.

A chef trying out a new recipe may not get it right on the first attempt. They might burn the dish or realize that the ingredients don't complement each other. Instead of giving up, they take notes, adjust the seasoning, and try again. Each mistake teaches them something new, helping them perfect the recipe over time.

Strategies for Adjusting Plans and Embracing Flexibility

In a rapidly changing world, rigid plans often become obsolete before they are even implemented. Flexibility is a key component of success because it allows us to adapt to new information, unexpected challenges, and changing circumstances. Being willing to adjust your plans based on feedback and experiences is a sign of strength, not weakness.

Proverbs 16:9 (NIV) offers valuable wisdom: *"In their hearts, humans plan their course, but the Lord establishes their steps."* This verse teaches us that while it's good to make plans, we must also be open to change and willing to follow a different path when God directs us.

A business owner launches a new product with a specific target market in mind. However, after receiving feedback, they realize that a different demographic is more interested in the product. Instead of sticking rigidly to the original plan, the owner pivots and adjusts their marketing strategy to reach the new audience. This flexibility leads to greater success than if they had refused to adapt.

Practical Tips for Embracing Flexibility:

1. **Be Open to Feedback:** Listen to what others are saying about your work or project. Use their insights to make improvements.

2. **Reevaluate Regularly:** Set aside time to review your progress and make necessary adjustments to your plan.

3. **Trust the Process:** Have faith that even if things don't go as planned, you are learning valuable lessons that will guide you forward.

Finding the balance between thoughtful planning and decisive action is crucial for achieving success. While it's important to think through our decisions and prepare adequately, overthinking and perfectionism can paralyze us and prevent us from making progress. Remember, action is the bridge that connects our plans to our goals. As you take steps forward, be willing to learn from your mistakes and adjust your course as needed. Trust that God will guide your steps and lead you toward the fulfillment of your purpose. Embrace flexibility, take action, and watch as your small steps lead to significant progress.

CHAPTER 6: STRATEGIES TO OVERCOME OVERTHINKING

Recognize the Triggers of Overthinking

The first step in overcoming overthinking is to recognize the situations or thoughts that trigger it. Overthinking often begins subtly, but once we become aware of our patterns, we can start to disrupt the cycle before it takes over. Some common triggers of overthinking include:

1. **Fear of Failure:**

   Many people overthink because they are afraid of making mistakes. They worry about what could go wrong and get stuck in a loop of "what if" scenarios. This fear stems from a desire to avoid disappointment or judgment from others.

2. **Uncertainty and Lack of Control:**

When we face situations that are uncertain or beyond our control, our minds often try to compensate by overanalyzing. We think that if we can anticipate every outcome, we might regain a sense of control. However, this mindset only leads to anxiety and rumination.

3. **Perfectionism:**
The need to be perfect can trigger overthinking. Perfectionists tend to obsess over details, fearing that any imperfection will lead to failure. This type of thinking prevents them from moving forward and making progress.

4. **Negative Past Experiences:**

Past traumas or negative experiences can serve as triggers for overthinking. When faced with a similar situation, the mind replays old scenarios, analyzing what happened and how it could have been different.

A person preparing for a job interview might find themselves replaying past interviews where they felt they didn't perform well. Instead of focusing on preparing for the upcoming opportunity, they get stuck analyzing their previous mistakes, which increases their anxiety.

To combat overthinking, start by noticing when you feel the urge to overanalyze. Pay attention to your thoughts and recognize if they are becoming repetitive or focused on worst-case scenarios. James 1:5 (NIV) says, *"If any of you lacks wisdom, you should ask God, who gives generously to all without finding fault, and it will be given to you."* Instead of relying solely on your own analysis, seek divine guidance and wisdom when faced with uncertainty.

Practical Techniques to Curb Overthinking

1. Mindfulness and Grounding Exercises

Mindfulness is the practice of bringing your attention to the present moment, without judgment. It helps break the cycle of overthinking by shifting your focus away from past regrets or future worries and grounding you in the "now." When you practice mindfulness, you become aware of your thoughts but do not allow them to control you.

Example Exercise: Deep Breathing for Grounding

- Sit comfortably, close your eyes, and take a deep breath in through your nose, filling your lungs.

- Hold the breath for a moment, then slowly exhale through your mouth.

- As you breathe, focus on the sensation of the air entering and leaving your body. This simple exercise can help you return to the present moment and interrupt overthinking.

Philippians 4:6-7 (NIV) encourages mindfulness: *"Do not be anxious about anything, but in every situation, by prayer and petition, with thanksgiving, present your requests to God. And the peace of God, which transcends all understanding, will guard your hearts and your minds in Christ Jesus."* This scripture reminds us to focus on God's peace rather than our worries.

2. Journaling Thoughts to Gain Clarity

Journaling is an effective tool for curbing overthinking because it allows you to release your thoughts onto paper, creating distance between you and the worries that occupy your mind. When you write down your thoughts, you can better organize them, identify patterns, and gain insights that might not be evident when the thoughts are just swirling in your head.

At the end of each day, take a few minutes to write down what's on your mind. Start by listing any worries or concerns you have. Then, write a possible action step for each concern or acknowledge if it's something you can't control. This practice helps clear your mind and reduces the urge to overthink.

3. The "5-Second Rule" for Taking Quick Action

The "5-Second Rule," popularized by Mel Robbins, is a simple but powerful technique for overcoming hesitation and overthinking. The idea is that when you have an impulse to act on a goal, you have five seconds before your mind starts to talk you out of it. By counting backward from five and taking action immediately, you bypass the mental barriers that lead to overthinking.

If you find yourself hesitating to send an important email or make a phone call, count down from five (5-4-3-2-1) and then take action before your mind can come up with reasons to delay. This technique helps you push past the initial resistance and move forward.

Try using the "5-Second Rule" whenever you notice yourself procrastinating or hesitating. It's a quick way to break the cycle of overthinking and get into action mode.

While practical techniques can help curb overthinking, it's also important to recognize the deeper mindset that often underlies chronic indecision and self-doubt. Let's explore the role of the 'overthinker impostor' and how it might be influencing your thoughts and actions.

The Overthinker Impostor: A Self-Sabotaging Persona

The "overthinker impostor" is a hidden persona that often masquerades as careful analysis or thorough preparation. In reality, this mindset is a form of self-sabotage, driven by fear and self-doubt. The overthinker impostor convinces us that we need to endlessly analyze every detail, seek perfection, and avoid taking risks, all under the guise of "being cautious." However, this mindset actually holds us back from making decisions, moving forward, and embracing new opportunities.

How the Overthinker Impostor Shows Up

1. **Chronic Indecision and the Fear of Making Mistakes**

   The overthinker impostor thrives on uncertainty, making us feel like we never have enough information to make a decision. It keeps us stuck in a loop of "what ifs," constantly questioning our choices and fearing the consequences of making a mistake.

   A job seeker might spend weeks debating whether to apply for a position because they worry they're not fully qualified. The overthinker impostor whispers, "You don't have all the skills yet; better wait until you're more prepared." As a result, they miss the application deadline and lose the opportunity altogether.

2. **Seeking Perfection as a Way to Avoid Action**

   Perfectionism is a key trait of the overthinker impostor. It convinces us that everything must be flawless before we can take the next step. This mindset leads to endless revisions and delays, preventing us from ever finishing what we start.

An artist working on a painting might keep making small changes, never feeling satisfied with the final product. The overthinker impostor tells them, "It's not perfect yet. You need to make a few more adjustments before showing it to anyone." This cycle can continue indefinitely, preventing the artist from sharing their work.

Strategies for Recognizing the Overthinker Impostor

Recognizing when the overthinker impostor is at play is the first step to overcoming it. Here are some common signs to look out for:

- You constantly second-guess your decisions, even after making a choice.

- You delay taking action because you feel you need more information or preparation.

- You seek external validation for every decision, doubting your own judgment.

- You fixate on minor details, avoiding the bigger picture or final outcome.

Practical Tools for Overcoming the Overthinker Impostor

1. **Challenge the Impostor with Action:**

   The best way to silence the overthinker impostor is by taking small, decisive actions, even if they feel imperfect. Each step forward builds momentum and reduces the power of self-doubt.

   If you're hesitating to start a new project because you feel unprepared, commit to spending just 10 minutes on it today. Taking that small action helps break the cycle of indecision and starts building confidence.

2. **Embrace the "Good Enough" Mindset:**

   Perfectionism feeds the overthinker impostor, so it's crucial to adopt a "good enough" mindset. Instead of striving for flawlessness, aim for progress and completion. Remind yourself that done is better than perfect.

When writing an email, set a timer for 10 minutes. Once the time is up, send the email without overanalyzing every word. Trust that your message is clear enough and focus on the next task.

2 Timothy 1:7 (NIV) encourages us: "*For the Spirit God gave us does not make us timid, but gives us power, love, and self-discipline.*" This verse reminds us that self-doubt and fear are not from God. By trusting in the spirit of power and self-discipline, we can overcome the grip of the overthinker impostor.

3. **Reframe Self-Doubt as Curiosity:**

Instead of letting self-doubt spiral into overthinking, reframe it as an opportunity for growth and exploration. Ask yourself, "What can I learn from this situation?" or "What's one small step I can take to find out more?" This shift in mindset helps transform fear into curiosity and action.

If you're worried about making a mistake during a presentation, reframe your anxiety by thinking, "This is a chance to learn more about public speaking. Even if I stumble, I'll gain valuable experience that I can use next time."

The overthinker impostor is a sneaky voice that often disguises itself as careful planning or thoughtful analysis. However, by recognizing its self-sabotaging patterns and challenging them with decisive action, you can break free from chronic indecision and start living more confidently. Remember, true wisdom comes from trusting in both your abilities and in God's guidance. As Psalm 56:3 (NIV) says, *"When I am afraid, I put my trust in you."* Trust yourself, take the next step, and watch the overthinker impostor fade away.

The Role of Positive Self-Talk and Affirmations

Overthinking is often fueled by negative self-talk and internal criticism. When we constantly tell ourselves things like, "I'm not good enough," or "I always mess up," we reinforce a cycle of self-doubt. Positive self-talk and affirmations are powerful tools for countering these negative thoughts and building a healthier, more empowering mindset.

In Proverbs 18:21 (NIV), it says, "*The tongue has the power of life and death, and those who love it will eat its fruit.*" This verse highlights the importance of the words we speak, even to ourselves. By choosing to speak positively, we can change the way we think and feel.

Example of Positive Affirmations:

- "I am capable of handling whatever comes my way."

- "I trust myself to make the right decisions."

- "Every step I take brings me closer to my goals."

A person who tends to overthink before giving a presentation might replace thoughts like, "I'm going to fail," with affirmations such as, "I am prepared, and I know my material well." This shift in self-talk helps to reduce anxiety and build confidence.

Make a habit of writing down a few positive affirmations each morning. Speak them out loud, even if you don't fully believe them at first. Over time, these positive statements will start to reshape your thought patterns and reduce the impulse to overthink.

Overthinking is a common challenge, but it can be managed with the right strategies. By recognizing your triggers, practicing mindfulness, using tools like journaling and the "5-Second Rule," and replacing negative self-talk with positive affirmations, you can break the cycle of overthinking. Remember, God has given us the ability to choose our thoughts and to live with a spirit of peace, not fear. Philippians 4:8 (NIV) sums it up well: "*Finally, brothers and sisters, whatever is true, whatever is noble, whatever is right, whatever is pure, whatever is lovely, whatever is admirable—if anything is excellent or praiseworthy—think about such things.*" Focus your mind on what is positive and productive, and you will find it easier to overcome the habit of overthinking.

In addition to using positive self-talk and mindfulness exercises, another effective strategy for managing overthinking is scheduling dedicated 'worry time.' Let's explore how this technique can help contain ruminative thoughts and reduce anxiety.

Practical Exercise: Scheduling "Worry Time"

One of the most challenging aspects of overthinking is the feeling that your worries are constantly intruding on your thoughts, making it hard to focus or relax. Instead of trying to suppress these thoughts (which often makes them stronger), you can contain them by scheduling specific "worry time." This technique involves setting aside a dedicated block of time each day to acknowledge and address your worries, allowing you to put them aside for the rest of the day.

Scheduling "worry time" gives your brain permission to worry, but only within a set time frame. By doing this, you create a mental boundary that helps prevent ruminative thoughts from taking over your entire day. This method is effective because it reduces the impulse to constantly engage with anxious thoughts, knowing that you will address them later during your designated time.

If you find yourself worrying throughout the day, schedule 15-20 minutes in the evening as your "worry time." During this period, sit down with a notepad and write down all the worries on your mind. Once the time is up, close the notebook and tell yourself that you've addressed your concerns for the day. If a worry pops up outside of this time, remind yourself that you'll handle it during your next scheduled session.

Step-by-Step Guide to Implementing "Worry Time":

1. **Choose a Specific Time and Duration:**

   Decide on a consistent time each day for your worry session. It could be in the evening after work or a quiet moment before bedtime. Limit the session to 15-20 minutes to avoid getting stuck in rumination.

   Set aside "worry time" from 7:30 to 7:50 PM each day. Use a timer to keep yourself on track.

2. **Create a Worry List:**

   During your scheduled time, write down all the worries and concerns that come to mind. Be honest and let your thoughts flow without judgment. This process helps externalize your worries, making them feel less overwhelming.

Write down specific worries like, "I'm worried about an upcoming deadline," or, "I'm concerned about my financial situation."

3. **Assess and Problem-Solve (If Needed):**

After listing your worries, take a moment to assess whether any of them require immediate action. If there's a practical step you can take to address a concern, write it down as a to-do item. For worries that are hypothetical or beyond your control, acknowledge them and let them go.

If you're worried about a project at work, note a specific action you can take tomorrow, such as, "Email my supervisor for clarification." For a worry like, "What if something goes wrong next week?" simply acknowledge it and remind yourself that it's a hypothetical scenario you can't control right now.

4. **End the Session and Refocus on the Present:**

Once your worry time is over, put your list away and shift your focus back to the present. Tell yourself that you've dedicated time to your concerns and that it's time to move on. If a worry resurfaces outside of your scheduled time, gently remind yourself that it can wait until the next session.

Matthew 6:34 (NIV) advises, "*Therefore do not worry about tomorrow, for tomorrow will worry about itself. Each day has enough trouble of its own.*" This verse reminds us of the importance of living in the present moment and not letting future worries consume us. Scheduling "worry time" aligns with this wisdom by containing our concerns to a specific time rather than allowing them to dominate our thoughts throughout the day.

Why "Worry Time" Is Effective

The technique of scheduling "worry time" works because it helps your brain feel acknowledged without being overwhelmed. When you give yourself a dedicated time to address your concerns, you're less likely to ruminate throughout the day. It also trains your mind to recognize that not every worry requires immediate attention, helping you build a healthier relationship with your thoughts.

A student might find themselves worrying constantly about an upcoming exam. By scheduling "worry time" each evening, they can list their concerns about the test and make a specific study plan. This process reduces their anxiety during the day because they know they have a set time to address their worries and prepare.

Combine "worry time" with other strategies like journaling or mindfulness. For instance, after writing down your worries, take a few deep breaths and practice a quick mindfulness exercise to help refocus your mind on the present.

Scheduling "worry time" is a simple yet powerful tool for managing overthinking. By containing your worries to a specific time each day, you can free up mental space for more productive and positive thoughts. Remember, it's not about ignoring your concerns but rather addressing them in a structured way that reduces their hold over you. As Philippians 4:6 (NIV) says, "*Do not be anxious about anything, but in every situation, by prayer and petition, with thanksgiving, present your requests to God.*" Let your worries be known during your dedicated time, and then trust in the process and in God's peace.

CHAPTER 7: CULTIVATING A MINDSET FOR GROWTH AND ACTION

Embracing the Mindset of a Thinker and a Doer

A growth-oriented mindset requires us to find the balance between being a thinker and a doer. Thoughtful reflection involves analyzing situations, understanding context, and planning carefully, while decisive action is about making choices and executing plans swiftly. When these two approaches are combined, they create a powerful synergy that can lead to significant personal and professional growth.

James 2:17 (NIV) states, *"In the same way, faith by itself, if it is not accompanied by action, is dead."* This verse highlights the importance of pairing our thoughts and intentions with action. It's not enough to have good ideas; we must also be willing to act on them. True growth comes from the ability to reflect thoughtfully and then move forward with confidence, even when the outcome is uncertain.

Consider an inventor who has an idea for a new product. They might spend time researching the market, identifying potential problems, and refining the design. This thoughtful reflection is essential for creating a viable product. However, if the inventor never takes the next step to create a prototype or launch the product, the idea remains just a concept. By balancing reflection with action, they bring their vision to life and contribute something valuable to the world. Here are some examples of historical and contemporary figures who embody this mindset:

1. Leonardo da Vinci: The Ultimate Thinker and Doer Leonardo da Vinci was a master at balancing deep thought with creative action. He was known for his notebooks filled with sketches, inventions, and scientific observations. Da Vinci spent a great deal of time studying anatomy, physics, and art, reflecting deeply on the natural world. However, he also translated his reflections into tangible works, such as paintings like the *Mona Lisa* and engineering designs for futuristic inventions. Da Vinci's ability to think deeply and then act on his ideas made him a true Renaissance man, leaving a lasting legacy in multiple fields.

2. Elon Musk: The Modern Thinker and Doer In the contemporary world, Elon Musk exemplifies the balance between reflection and action. Musk's approach to innovation involves both rigorous thinking and bold action. He has repeatedly demonstrated the ability to envision the future—whether through electric cars, space exploration, or sustainable energy—and then take decisive steps to make that vision a reality. Musk's mindset emphasizes the importance of taking calculated risks and learning through action, rather than getting stuck in analysis paralysis.

To cultivate this balanced mindset, set aside time for reflection but also commit to taking action within a specific timeframe. For instance, after planning a project, make a point to execute a small part of it immediately. This practice builds momentum and helps bridge the gap between thinking and doing.

To fully embrace the mindset of a thinker and a doer, it's essential to build a strong foundation of self-trust. Let's explore how developing self-trust can help reduce overthinking and boost your confidence in taking decisive action.

Building Self-Trust: The Foundation of a Growth Mindset

Developing a growth mindset requires more than just the willingness to think deeply and take action—it also demands a strong sense of self-trust. When you trust yourself, you are less likely to fall into the trap of overthinking, second-guessing every decision, or hesitating to take the next step. Self-trust is the belief that you can handle whatever comes your way, and it is built through consistent, intentional actions.

One of the most effective ways to build self-trust is by keeping small promises to yourself. Each time you set a goal and follow through, you reinforce your belief in your own abilities. These small wins accumulate over time, creating a strong foundation of confidence that helps you move forward without fear of failure.

If you commit to going for a 10-minute walk every morning, honor that promise. Even on days when you don't feel motivated, completing this small task sends a message to your subconscious mind: "I can trust myself to do what I say I will do." Over time, this practice builds self-trust and makes it easier to take on larger challenges.

Matthew 25:23 (NIV) says, *"His master replied, 'Well done, good and faithful servant! You have been faithful with a few things; I will put you in charge of many things.'"* This verse highlights the importance of being faithful in small commitments, suggesting that when we are consistent in the little things, we build the capacity for greater responsibilities.

Strategies for Building Self-Trust

1. Start with Small, Achievable Goals

Building self-trust begins with setting realistic, manageable goals. When you start small, you give yourself the chance to succeed consistently, which strengthens your belief in your own capabilities.

If you want to build a habit of reading daily, start with a goal of reading for just 5 minutes a day. As you consistently meet this goal, increase the time gradually. This approach helps you develop the habit without overwhelming yourself, reinforcing your ability to follow through.

2. Practice Self-Compassion When You Fall Short

Building self-trust doesn't mean you'll never make mistakes. It's about how you respond to those moments when you fall short. Instead of criticizing yourself, practice self-compassion and remind yourself that setbacks are a natural part of growth.

If you set a goal to exercise every day but miss a workout, don't berate yourself. Acknowledge it, forgive yourself, and commit to getting back on track the next day. This response builds resilience and maintains your self-trust.

3. Celebrate Your Wins—Big and Small

Take time to acknowledge your achievements, no matter how minor they may seem. Celebrating your successes, even small ones, reinforces your belief in your own abilities and encourages you to keep moving forward.

Keep a "win journal" where you note down every small promise you kept to yourself, such as completing a task on time or making a healthy choice. Reviewing this list regularly reminds you of your progress and strengthens your self-trust.

Philippians 4:13 (NIV) says, "*I can do all this through him who gives me strength.*" This verse emphasizes the importance of relying on God's strength while also trusting in the abilities He has given you. As you build self-trust, remember that it is rooted in the confidence that God is guiding your steps.

How Self-Trust Reduces Overthinking

When you trust yourself, you no longer feel the need to overanalyze every decision or seek constant reassurance. You become more comfortable with uncertainty and are willing to take risks, knowing that you can handle whatever outcome arises. This shift in mindset allows you to focus on action rather than getting stuck in a cycle of indecision.

A business owner facing a tough decision might usually spend hours analyzing every possible outcome, fearing they'll make the wrong choice. However, if they have built strong self-trust, they can make a decision more quickly and confidently, trusting their instincts and experience.

When you find yourself hesitating or second-guessing a choice, take a moment to pause and say, "I trust my ability to make the right decision." This simple affirmation can help break the cycle of overthinking and give you the confidence to move forward.

Building self-trust is an essential component of cultivating a growth mindset. By keeping promises to yourself, practicing self-compassion, and celebrating your wins, you lay the foundation for confidence and resilience. As your self-trust grows, you'll find it easier to embrace both reflection and action, moving forward with a clear mind and a courageous heart. Remember, trusting yourself is an extension of trusting the path that God has laid out for you. Proverbs 3:5-6 (NIV) reminds us, "Trust in the Lord with all your heart and lean not on your own understanding; in all your ways submit to him, and he will make your paths straight."

The Importance of Self-Compassion

Self-compassion is the practice of being kind and understanding toward oneself, especially in moments of failure or disappointment. It's about treating yourself with the same kindness you would offer a friend who is struggling. Many people fall into the trap of harsh self-criticism, which fuels overthinking and creates a cycle of self-doubt. When we are overly critical of ourselves, we become fearful of making mistakes, which hinders our willingness to take action and learn from new experiences.

Psalm 103:13-14 (NIV) offers a reminder of God's compassionate nature: "*As a father has compassion on his children, so the Lord has compassion on those who fear him; for he knows how we are formed, he remembers that we are dust.*" Just as God shows compassion towards us, we are called to show that same gentleness and grace towards ourselves.

A young musician preparing for a performance might make several mistakes during rehearsal. If they criticize themselves harshly, saying, "I'll never get this right," they might start overthinking every note, increasing their anxiety and negatively affecting their practice. However, if they choose to be kind to themselves and say, "It's okay to make mistakes while learning," they can move past the errors, adjust, and improve without getting stuck in self-doubt.

Self-compassion is a powerful antidote to overthinking because it interrupts the cycle of self-criticism that often fuels it. When we practice self-compassion, we acknowledge our imperfections without letting them define us. Instead of replaying our mistakes and focusing on what went wrong, we accept them as part of the growth process and move forward with a positive mindset.

Romans 8:1 (NIV) says, "*Therefore, there is now no condemnation for those who are in Christ Jesus.*" This verse reminds us that we are not condemned for our mistakes; instead, we are offered grace. When we internalize this truth, we can let go of excessive self-judgment and focus on growth.

Practical Tips for Practicing Self-Compassion:

1. **Acknowledge Your Feelings:** When you make a mistake or feel overwhelmed, pause and acknowledge your emotions without judgment. Simply say, "I'm feeling stressed right now, and that's okay."

2. **Practice Self-Kindness:** Speak to yourself with the same kindness you would offer a loved one. Replace harsh criticisms with encouraging words, such as, "I'm learning, and it's normal to make mistakes."

3. **Remember You Are Not Alone:** Recognize that everyone makes mistakes and experiences setbacks. You are part of a shared human experience, and it's normal to face challenges.

Imagine an entrepreneur whose first business venture fails. If they respond with self-compassion, they might say, "It's disappointing, but I've learned valuable lessons that I can apply to my next project." This mindset allows them to reflect on what went wrong without getting stuck in overthinking. Instead, they use the experience as a stepping stone for future success.

Cultivating a mindset for growth and action requires both the willingness to reflect deeply and the courage to take decisive steps forward. It also involves treating ourselves with compassion when we fall short. By embracing the mindset of a thinker and a doer, and by practicing self-compassion, we equip ourselves with the tools needed to overcome obstacles and achieve our goals. Remember the words of Philippians 3:13-14 (NIV): "*Forgetting what is behind and straining toward what is ahead, I press on toward the goal to win the prize for which God has called me heavenward in Christ Jesus.*" Let go of past mistakes, focus on what lies ahead, and move forward with confidence and kindness towards yourself.

CHAPTER 8: PUTTING IT ALL TOGETHER

Creating a Personal Action Plan

To live a balanced life that embraces thoughtful reflection without falling into overthinking, it's essential to have a practical action plan. This plan will serve as a guide to help you harness the power of your thoughts and channel them into meaningful actions. Here's a step-by-step guide to creating your personal action plan:

Step 1: Define Your Vision and Goals Start by identifying what you want to achieve. Take time to reflect on your vision for the future and set clear, specific goals. Proverbs 29:18 (NIV) states, *"Where there is no vision, the people perish."* Having a clear vision provides direction and motivation, helping you stay focused on your path.

If your goal is to start a new fitness routine, define what success looks like for you. It could be as specific as exercising three times a week or aiming to run a 5K within six months.

Step 2: Break Down Your Goals into Actionable Steps Divide your big goals into smaller, manageable tasks. This prevents you from becoming overwhelmed and reduces the tendency to overthink. Breaking tasks down into bite-sized steps helps you make steady progress and keeps you moving forward.

If your goal is to write a book, start by breaking it down into smaller tasks such as outlining the chapters, setting a daily word count goal, and scheduling time for writing each day.

Step 3: Set Deadlines and Milestones Establish deadlines for each step of your plan. Deadlines create a sense of urgency and help you stay on track. Set milestones to celebrate along the way, as they provide opportunities to acknowledge your progress and stay motivated.

If your goal is to save money for a vacation, set a deadline for reaching specific savings targets, such as saving $500 by the end of the first month.

Step 4: Prioritize and Take Action Determine which tasks are most important and start with those. Prioritization helps you focus on the actions that will have the biggest impact. James 4:17 (NIV) reminds us, *"If anyone, then, knows the good they ought to do and doesn't do it, it is sin for them."* This verse emphasizes the importance of taking action on what we know is right.

If your plan includes multiple tasks, prioritize the one that will move you closer to your goal the fastest. Instead of overthinking where to start, pick the task with the highest priority and take action immediately.

Accountability and Consistency

Staying consistent and holding yourself accountable are key elements of any successful plan. Without accountability, it's easy to fall back into old habits of overthinking and procrastination. Here are some practical tips for building consistency and accountability into your life:

1. **Track Your Progress:**

    Keep a record of your actions and accomplishments. Whether you use a journal, a planner, or a digital app, tracking your progress helps you see how far you've come and keeps you motivated to continue.

    If you are working towards a fitness goal, keep a log of your workouts, noting the exercises completed and how you felt afterward. This will help you stay aware of your progress and identify areas for improvement.

2. **Find an Accountability Partner:**

    Share your goals with a trusted friend or mentor who can help keep you on track. An accountability partner provides support, encouragement, and honest feedback, helping you stay committed to your plan.

    Ecclesiastes 4:9-10 (NIV) says, *"Two are better than one, because they have a good return for their labor: If either of them falls down, one can help the other up."* This scripture underscores the importance of having someone to support you in your journey.

If you are aiming to develop a new habit, such as daily meditation, ask a friend to check in with you each day to see how you're doing. Their encouragement will help you stay consistent.

3. **Build Routines and Habits:**

Consistency is easier to maintain when you establish routines and turn tasks into habits. By creating a routine, you reduce the mental effort required to make decisions, freeing up your mind for more important tasks.

If your goal is to read more, set a specific time each day for reading, such as right before bed. Over time, this routine will become a habit, making it easier to stick with.

Reflect, Adjust, and Move Forward

Reflection is a crucial part of growth. It allows you to assess your progress, learn from your experiences, and make adjustments to your plan. Regular reflection helps you stay aligned with your goals and prevents you from falling into the trap of overthinking.

2 Corinthians 13:5 (NIV) advises, *"Examine yourselves to see whether you are in the faith; test yourselves."* This scripture highlights the importance of self-examination and reflection as part of our spiritual journey. Similarly, reflecting on your goals and actions helps you stay true to your intentions and make informed decisions.

Step 1: Schedule Regular Check-Ins Set aside time each week or month to review your progress. During these check-ins, ask yourself the following questions:

- What progress have I made towards my goals?

- What challenges have I encountered, and how can I address them?

- Are there any adjustments I need to make to my plan?

A business owner might schedule a monthly review to evaluate their company's performance. They might look at sales numbers, customer feedback, and overall growth, using this information to adjust their strategy for the coming month.

Step 2: Be Open to Change Flexibility is key to adapting your plan based on new information or circumstances. Don't be afraid to make changes if something isn't working. Adjusting your plan doesn't mean you've failed; it means you're responding thoughtfully to the reality of the situation.

If you planned to exercise in the morning but find that it's not sustainable due to your schedule, switch to an evening workout routine instead. This small adjustment can make it easier to stick to your plan.

Step 3: Celebrate Wins and Learn from Mistakes Take time to celebrate your achievements, no matter how small. Recognizing your progress boosts your confidence and motivates you to keep going. At the same time, view your mistakes as learning opportunities rather than failures.

After completing a major project at work, take a moment to acknowledge your efforts and reflect on what went well. If there were areas that could have been improved, note them for next time but don't dwell on them. Use what you've learned to inform your next project.

Putting everything together requires a commitment to both planning and action. By creating a personal action plan, staying consistent, and reflecting regularly, you can achieve a balanced life that embraces both thoughtful reflection and decisive action. Remember, growth is a journey, not a destination. Philippians 3:13-14 (NIV) reminds us, *"Forgetting what is behind and straining toward what is ahead, I press on toward the goal to win the prize for which God has called me heavenward in Christ Jesus."* Keep pressing forward, adjusting as needed, and trusting that each step you take is leading you closer to your goals.

CONCLUSION: EMBRACE THOUGHT, EMBRACE ACTION

As we bring this journey to a close, let's take a moment to reflect on the powerful strategies we've explored to help you transform overthinking into meaningful action.

Reinforcing the New Strategies: From Reflection to Action

Throughout this book, we've examined the fine line between productive, deep thinking and the pitfalls of overthinking. By recognizing the difference, you can harness the power of your thoughts while taking decisive steps forward. Here's a recap of the new strategies we've added to help you break free from the cycle of overthinking and embrace a life of balanced reflection and purposeful action:

1. Reframing Overthinking as a Strength

We started by challenging the negative perception of overthinking, highlighting how deep thinking can be beneficial in certain contexts. When approached with intentionality, deep thought leads to insightful decisions and breakthroughs. The key is to differentiate it from unproductive rumination, which traps us in a cycle of self-doubt and worry.

2. Differentiating Deep Thinking from Overthinking

We provided clear criteria to help you identify when your thinking is productive versus when it turns into harmful overthinking. Using practical examples and a simple checklist, you now have the tools to recognize the shift and redirect your thoughts towards constructive reflection.

3. Understanding the Role of the Amygdala

We explored the brain's role in triggering anxiety during periods of overthinking, focusing on the amygdala's activation of the fight-or-flight response. By learning practical techniques such as mindful breathing and grounding exercises, you can calm your mind and reduce the physiological effects of overthinking.

4. Building Self-Trust

Self-trust emerged as a crucial foundation for overcoming overthinking. We introduced strategies for building self-trust, such as keeping small promises to yourself, practicing self-compassion, and celebrating your wins. Strengthening your self-trust reduces the tendency to second-guess your decisions and fosters a confident mindset.

5. Replacing Negative Thoughts Instead of Suppressing Them

Instead of attempting to suppress negative, anxious thoughts, we discussed the power of replacing them with positive affirmations and imagery. This technique helps you reframe your mindset and break free from the grip of perfectionism and self-doubt.

6. Scenarios Where Overthinking Is Useful vs. When It's Not

We distinguished between situations where deep thinking is beneficial—such as strategic planning and complex problem-solving—and when it becomes detrimental, like in daily decision-making. Understanding this balance allows you to engage in thoughtful reflection without getting trapped in indecision.

7. The Overthinker Impostor

We introduced the concept of the "overthinker impostor," a self-sabotaging persona that feeds on chronic indecision and perfectionism. By recognizing this mindset and challenging it with decisive action, you can overcome the fear-based habits that hold you back.

8. Scheduling "Worry Time"

The practical exercise of scheduling "worry time" offers a structured way to contain and address ruminative thoughts. By dedicating a specific time each day to acknowledge your concerns, you free up mental space and reduce the impulse to overthink throughout the day.

Embrace Thought, Embrace Action: Your Path Forward

The strategies we've covered in this book are designed to help you strike a healthy balance between deep, reflective thinking and bold, decisive action. Remember, your thoughts are powerful tools—but only when they are directed with purpose and intention. By harnessing the positive aspects of deep thinking while avoiding the traps of overthinking, you can live a life of clarity, confidence, and meaningful progress.

Proverbs 16:3 (NIV) advises, "*Commit to the Lord whatever you do, and he will establish your plans.*" This verse reminds us to trust not only in our own abilities but also in God's guidance as we navigate the journey from thought to action. When you align your intentions with faith, you can step forward with the assurance that you are on the right path.

It's time to take what you've learned and put it into practice. No longer confined by the limitations of overthinking, you have the tools to transform your thoughts into meaningful action. Whether it's pursuing a new goal, making a bold decision, or embracing a new challenge, trust in yourself and in the process.

Remember, the journey from thought to action is not about achieving perfection—it's about progress. Embrace your unique strengths, take that first step, and watch as your confidence grows. As Philippians 4:13 (NIV) says, "*I can do all this through him who gives me strength.*" With each thoughtful reflection and decisive action, you are creating the life you were meant to live.

Think it, do it, and live it.

The Main Takeaways from the Book

As we bring this journey to a close, let's reflect on the core principles discussed throughout the book. We started by exploring the difference between productive thinking and the pitfalls of overthinking, recognizing that while deep thought can lead to great insights, excessive analysis can hinder progress and steal our peace. We've learned that:

1. **Thinking Is Good, But Overthinking Is Not:**

   Thoughtful reflection allows us to make wise decisions, but overthinking leads to confusion, anxiety, and inaction. By understanding the triggers of overthinking, we can start to break free from its grip.

2. **Embrace Your Uniqueness and Find Your Balance:**

   Each of us has unique strengths and approaches to problem-solving. Whether you lean more towards deep thinking or instinctive action, embracing your individuality is key. Balancing thoughtful reflection with decisive action allows you to harness your full potential.

3. **Perfectionism Is the Enemy of Progress:**

   Striving for perfection often leads to procrastination and stagnation. Instead of aiming for flawlessness, focus on making steady progress. Accept mistakes as part of the growth process and use them as learning opportunities.

4. **Take Action, Even If It's Imperfect:**

Action is the bridge between your thoughts and your goals. Waiting for the perfect moment or solution can lead to analysis paralysis. Instead, take small, actionable steps, learn as you go, and be willing to adjust your plans.

5. **Cultivate Self-Compassion and Flexibility:**

Being kind to yourself when you make mistakes is essential for growth. Self-compassion helps you recover from setbacks without getting trapped in a cycle of self-criticism. Additionally, staying flexible allows you to adapt to new challenges and opportunities as they arise.

Finding a Healthy Balance Between Thinking and Taking Action

Finding the right balance between thinking and doing is at the heart of living a fulfilled and productive life. Thoughtful reflection provides clarity, while action turns ideas into reality. Ecclesiastes 3:1 (NIV) says, *"There is a time for everything, and a season for every activity under the heavens."* This verse reminds us that there is a time to think and a time to act, and wisdom lies in knowing when to do each.

The key to success is not to eliminate thinking or action but to find a harmonious rhythm between the two. When we spend too much time in our heads, we miss out on opportunities for growth and experience. Conversely, if we act without reflection, we risk making hasty decisions that may not align with our values or goals.

Consider a ship captain navigating through uncertain waters. The captain must take time to study the map and assess the weather conditions (thoughtful reflection), but they must also make timely decisions to steer the ship (decisive action). Both thinking and action are necessary to reach the destination safely.

The world is full of possibilities and experiences waiting to be discovered. Overthinking keeps us confined within the walls of our minds, but stepping out and taking action allows us to engage fully with life. It's time to embrace both your thoughts and your actions, to dream big, and then take the necessary steps to bring those dreams to fruition.

Romans 12:2 (NIV) encourages us: "*Do not conform to the pattern of this world, but be transformed by the renewing of your mind.*" This transformation begins when we free ourselves from the patterns of overthinking and embrace a mindset of growth, action, and faith.

A Call to Action:

- **Dream Boldly:** Allow yourself to think deeply and envision the possibilities. Your thoughts are powerful tools for shaping your future.

- **Act Decisively:** Don't let fear or doubt hold you back. Take the first step, even if it feels small, and trust that God is guiding your path.

- **Reflect and Adjust:** As you move forward, take time to reflect on your experiences. Learn from your mistakes, celebrate your successes, and make adjustments as needed.

Remember, life is a journey that requires both the power of thought and the courage of action. Embrace the wisdom of thoughtful reflection, but don't be afraid to take decisive steps. The path to growth, fulfillment, and success lies in finding the right balance. As you step out of your head and into the world, may you walk with confidence, guided by faith and purpose.

Philippians 4:13 (NIV) serves as a fitting conclusion: "*I can do all this through him who gives me strength.*" With God's strength and your balanced mindset, there is nothing you cannot achieve. Embrace your thoughts, take action, and live the life you were meant to live.

ABOUT THE AUTHOR

Nick Imoru is a dynamic speaker, author, educator, entrepreneur, and consultant based in Canada. He is the President of Achievers Centre, a division of Philips Reliability Consult Inc. Nick's mission is centered on empowering the human spirit through consulting, coaching, connecting and circulating ideas and information. His goal is to inspire, ignite passion, create profit, and make a spiritual impact, ultimately helping individuals bridge the gap between where they are and where they aspire to be.

Nick holds a B.Eng. in Mechanical and Production Engineering and an MSc. in Advanced Technology from the UK. With over 18 years of experience in the Oil and Gas industry, he specializes in Maintenance & Reliability Engineering and is a Certified Maintenance & Reliability Professional (CMRP), reflecting his commitment to excellence in his field.

As the author of over 20 books and numerous articles and research papers, Nick's work spans personal development, spirituality, academia, business, and finance. He is the founder of Achievers Consult, Achievers Centre, and Achievers Publishing, all operating under Philips Reliability Consult Inc.

Nick is happily married to Dr. Margaret and is a proud father of two daughters, Nelly and Myra. His unwavering dedication to personal and professional growth, combined with his entrepreneurial spirit, continues to make a profound impact on individuals and organizations, guiding them towards success and fulfillment.

With a vision to inspire, train, develop, and unlock potential, Nick Imoru is committed to helping individuals and businesses achieve their highest levels of success.

To contact Nick or learn more about Achievers Centre, opportunities, speeches, and seminars, please use the information below:

Email: Nick@achieverscentre.com
Website: www.achieverscentre.com

BOOKS BY SAME AUTHOR

- A Heart for God
- Operating God's Private Lines
- Growing In Life
- Money & Pleasure: Trap of Purpose
- Success Buttons for Life & Academic Excellence
- The Making of Greatness
- Your Best Year Ever
- Nothing Just Happens
- How Did I Become Like This
- Achievers Daily Tonic
- Living in His Fullness: Unveiling the Life, Mission, Death and Triumph of Jesus
- Your Belief System: How Your Thoughts Dictate Your Life
- The Wit & Wisdom of Dr David Oyedepo
- The Tongue: How Your Words Shape Your Destiny

- He Has Said...So We May Boldly Say
- Kings Don't Beg, They Make Decrees
- Character: The Blueprint for a Great Future
- Living in His Light: Understanding Your New Identity in Christ
- Personal & Family Budgeting: Mastering Your Money for Financial Freedom
- Your Money, Your Future: A Student's Guide to Financial Success
- Choosing the Right Path: A Career Guide for Teens and Youth
- The 21 Life Rules Every Child Should Live By
- Saving Your Future: A Practical Guide to Financial Literacy
- The Power of Your Environment: How Your Surroundings Shape Your Life
- Adventures in God's Amazing Storybook, Part 1
- Adventures in God's Amazing Storybook, Part 2

To order any of these books, please visit:

Our online shop @ www.achieverscentre.com

or any of the amazon websites:

www.amazon.ca or www.amazon.com

www.amazon.co.uk, etc

www.ingramcontent.com/pod-product-compliance
Lightning Source LLC
Chambersburg PA
CBHW050004040726
47599CB00014B/1208